*Newfoundland
and
Labrador
Lighthouses
by Harold Stiver*

Copyright Statement

**Newfoundland and Labrador Lighthouses
A Guide for Photographers and Explorers**

Published by Harold Stiver
Copyright 2025 Harold Stiver

License Notes
All rights reserved. No part of this book may be reproduced in any form or by any electronic or mechanical means including information storage and retrieval systems without permission in writing from the author, except by the reviewer who may quote brief passages
Version 1.0
ISBN#978-1-927835-55-5

Table of Contents

A Short History of Lighthouses   7
Newfoundland and Labrador Map   9

Lighthouses

Bacalhao Island	10
Baccalieu Island	11
Baccalieu Island Southwest Point	77
Bay Bulls	12
Bear Cove Point (Fermuse)	77
Bell Island	13
Belle Island North End	14
Belle Island South End Lower	15
Belle Island South End Upper	15
Boar Island	16
Brigus	17
Broad Cove Point Range Front	18
Burnt Point	19
Cabot Islands	20
Camp Islands	21
Cape Anguille	22
Cape Bauld	23
Cape Bonavista	24
Cape Norman	25
Cape Pine	26
Cape Race	27
Cape Ray	28
Cape Spear (new)	29
Cape Spear (old)	30
Cape St Francis	31
Cape St. Mary's	32
Channel Head	33
Colombier Islands	77
Conche	77
Cow Head	34
Dawson Point	35
Double Island	36
English Harbour West	37
Ferryland Head	38
Flowers Cove	39
Fort Amherst	40
Fort Point (Admiral's Point)	41

Fortune Head	42
Fox Point (Fishing Point)	43
François Bay (West Point)	44
Garnish	45
Grand Bank Wharf	46
Green Island (Catalina)	47
Green Island (Fortune Bay)	77
Green Point	48
Gull Island (Cape St. John)	49
Hants Harbour	50
Harbour Point (Sandy Point)	51
Heart's Content	52
Keppel Island	53
Kings Cove Head	54
La Haye Point	77
Little Denier Island	55
Lobster Cove Head	56
Long Point (Twillingate)	57
Manuel Island	58
Marticot Island	77
Middle Head	59
New Férolle Peninsula	60
North Penguin Island	77
Northwest Head (Ramea)	61
Offer Wadham Island	62
Pass Island	77
Peckford Island	63
Point Amour	64
Point Riche	65
Point Verde	66
Powles Head	67
Puffin Island	68
Random Head Harbour	69
Rocky Point (Harbour Breton)	70
Rose Blanche	71
Saddle Island (Red Bay)	77
Salmon Point	78
St. Jacques Island	72
St. Modeste Island	73
Surgeon Cove Point	78
Tides Cove Point	74
Westport Cove	75
Woody Point	76

Tours
Labrador Tour	79
Northern Newfoundland Tour1	80
Northern Newfoundland Tour2	81
Northern Newfoundland Tour3	82
South Newfoundland Tour1	83
South Newfoundland Tour2	84
St. John's Tour	85
Glossary	86
Photo Credits	90
The Photographer's and Explorer's Series	91
Index	93

A Short History of Lighthouses

There is some evidence of a lighthouse from the 5th century B.C. of Themistocles of Athens constructing a stone column with a fire on top. This was at the harbour of Piraeus, associated with Athens.

However one of most famous and spectacular early structures was the Lighthouse of Alexandria, or the Pharos of Alexandria. It was one of the Seven Wonders of the Ancient World.

The lighthouse was built in the Third Century B.C. in Alexandria, Egypt by Ptolemy II. It stood on the island of Pharos in the harbour of Alexandria and was said to be 110 metres (350 feet) high.

The lighthouse was built in three stages, a large square at the bottom, an octagonal layer in the middle, and a cylindrical tower at the top.

The structure lasted until a series of earthquakes damaged it, with the 1303 Crete earthquake resulting in its destruction.

The Tower of Hercules, in northwest Spain, is modelled after the Pharos Lighthouse. It is the world's oldest surviving lighthouse.

The first lighthouse in Canada was built in 1734 in Louisbourg on Cape Breton Island, Nova Scotia. Over the years, the structure was damaged beyond repair in a battle between the British and the French in 1758, destroyed by fire in 1923 and had to be rebuilt several times. The lighthouse known today was built in 1923.

Currently Canada's oldest surviving lighthouse is Sambro Island Lighthouse, built in 1758 at the entrance to Halifax Harbour. It is seen in the image above.

The oldest surviving lighthouse in Newfoundland is the Cape Spear Lighthouse which opened in 1836. It serves as the chief main approach light for St. John's harbour . It is a stone tower surrounded by the dwelling which was constructed by local builders Nicolas Croke and William Parker.

Cape Spear, Newfoundland's oldest surviving lighthouse, has served as the chief approach light for St. John's harbour since 1836. Constructed by local builders Nicolas Croke and William Parker, it consists of a stone tower surrounded by a frame residence, a common lighthouse design on Canada's east coast. The site was listed as a National Historic Site in 1962. Parks Canada began a 5 year restoration of the lighthouse in 1977 and the Cape Spear National Historic Park was opened by Prince Charles and Princess Diana in 1983.

Newfoundland and Labrador Maps

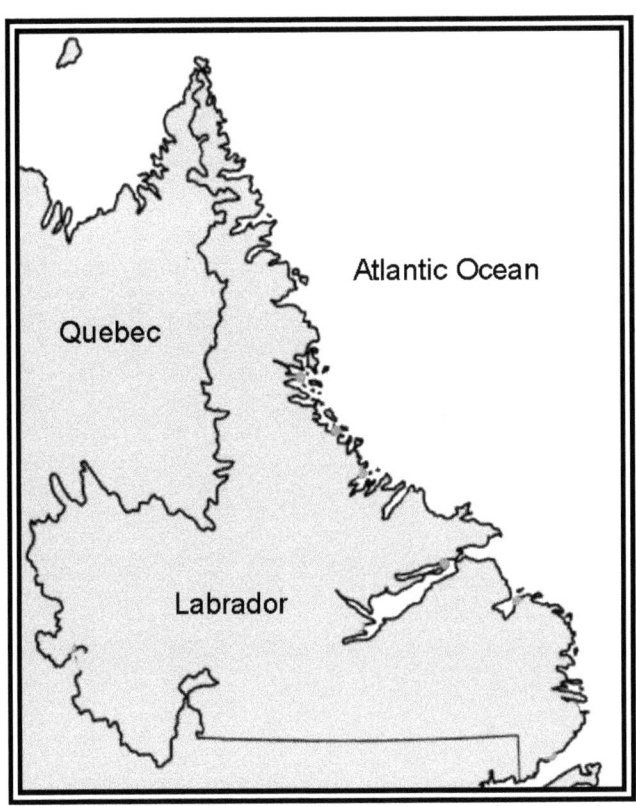

Bacalhao Island Light

The Bacalhao Island Lighthouse was opened in 1894 on the southwest corner of the island. The dwelling was built nearby with a covered walkway to the tower. In 1924 the lens was upgraded from sixth-order to fourth-order. A fog alarm building and a new dwelling were built on the island in the early 1960s. The iron tower was listed as a Federal Heritage Building in 1989.

Description: Circular tower with red and white spiral bands

Location: Bacalhao Island

Directions: Accessible by boat

Coordinates: 49°41'12.8"N 54°33'24.6"W

Opened: 1894

Automated: 1929

Deactivated: Active

Height: 14 meters, 45 feet

Focal Height: 106 meters, 348 feet

Signal: White flash every 10 seconds

Foghorn signal: Blast every 30 seconds

Visitor Access: Grounds open, tower closed

Baccalieu Island Lighthouse

In 1840 the Commissioners of Lighthouses called for a light on Baccalieu Island but it wasn't until 1859 before the Baccalieu Island Lighthouse was opened. The contract was fulfilled by John T. Nevill. A square, two-storey keepers' dwelling was connected to the tower by a covered passageway. The site is one the most important for breeding seabirds and is closed from April 1 to October 30. In the early 1990s, a skeleton tower was erected by the original tower and the brick tower was deactivated

Description: Inactive circular red brick tower by active skeleton tower

Location: Red Head Cove

Directions: Accessible by boat

Coordinates: 48°08'59.6"N 52°47'53.2"W

Opened: Original 1859, skeleton tower 1990s

Automated: 1963

Deactivated: Active skeleton tower by inactive original tower

Height: 13.5 meters, 45 feet

Focal Height: 166 meters, 544 feet

Signal: White flash every 6 seconds

Foghorn signal: Blast every 60 seconds

Visitor Access: Grounds open outside of breeding season, tower closed

Bay Bulls (Bull Head) Lighthouse

The Bay Bulls (Bull Head) Lighthouse was opened in 1908. It was located on the north side of the entrance to Bay Bulls Harbour. It is a circular tower covered with cast iron. The lighthouse was listed as a Recognized Federal Heritage Building in 1992.

Description: White, conical cast iron tower

Location: Bay Bulls

Directions: Accessible by a hike of 5 km (3 mi) on the Spout Path from Bay Bulls

Coordinates: 47°18'38.7"N 52°44'48.6"W

Opened: 1908

Automated: 1931

Deactivated: Active

Height: 11.5 meters, 38 feet

Focal Height: 60 meters, 197 feet

Signal: White flash every 6 seconds

Foghorn Signal: N/A

Visitor Access: Grounds open, tower closed

Bell Island Lighthouse

Bell Island is the largest island in Conception Bay. The Dominion Steel Company requested the building of a lighthouse there to aid shipping transporting iron ore from the island. In 1940 the Bell Island Lighthouse opened with the tower keepers dwelling and a fog alarm building. The original tower was replaced in 1966 due to erosion and was moved inland in 2004 for the same reason.

Description: Square cylindrical wood tower

Location: Wabana

Directions: From Wabana, head NW on Fitzgeralds Ln for 600 meters and turn left onto Quigleys Line. After 350 meters, turn right onto Lighthouse Rd where the site is 1.2 km

Coordinates: 47°39'18.0"N 52°54'59.3"W

Opened: 1966

Automated: Still staffed

Deactivated: Active

Height: 9 meters, 30 feet

Focal Height: 53 meters, 173 feet

Signal: White flash every 6 seconds

Foghorn Signal: 3 second blast every 30 seconds

Visitor Access: Grounds open, tower closed

Belle Island North End Lighthouse

In 1905 the Belle Isle North End Lighthouse was opened as an aid to ships travelling the northern route through the Strait of Belle Isle. In 1908 six flying buttresses were added for increased stability. The tower was deactivated in 2005 and a skeleton tower replaced it. The lighthouse was listed as a Recognized Federal Heritage Building in 1989.

Description: Dodecagonal tower with six flying buttress

Location: Belle Isle

Directions: Accessible by boat

Coordinates: 52°00'48.9"N 55°16'49.3"W

Opened: Original 1905, light replaced by skeleton tower 2004

Automated: 1976

Deactivated: 2004

Height: 27 meters, 89 feet

Focal Height: 42 meters, 138 feet

Signal: White flash every 11 seconds

Foghorn Signal: Blast every 30 seconds

Visitor Access: Grounds open, tower closed

Belle Island South End Range Lights

\Both of the Range Lights continue to be active with each showing a white flash every 20 seconds. The lower lighthouse, upper lighthouse, and keepers' duplex were listed as a Recognized Federal Heritage Buildings in 1990

Lower Range (Image above)

Description: White cylindrical concrete tower.

Location: Quirpon

Directions: Accessible by boat

Coordinates: 51°52'38.0"N 55°23'03.0"W

Opened: 1880

Automated: 1969

Deactivated: Active

Height: 7 meters, 23 feet

Focal Height: 30 meters, 100 feet

Signal: White flash every 20 seconds

Foghorn signal: Fog alarm was located to the upper lighthouse in 1912

Visitor Access: Closed

Upper Range

Description: White, conical limestone tower

Location: Quirpon

Directions: Accessible by boat

Coordinates: 51°52'48.1"N 55°22'54.4"W

Opened: 1858

Automated: 1969

Deactivated: Active

Height: 19 meters, 62 feet

Focal Height: 137 meters, 450 feet

Signal: White flash every 20 seconds

Visitor Access: Closed

Boar Island Lighthouse

The original Boar Island Lighthouse was built by Joseph Whiddon and opened in 1874. The structure was destroyed in a fire in 1946. A square, metal, skeletal tower was sending the signal in 2009.

Description: Skeleton tower

Location: Burgeo

Directions: Accessible by boat

Coordinates: 47°36'23.2"N 57°35'12.2"W

Opened: Original 1874, Current 2009

Automated: 2009

Deactivated: Active

Height: 10 meters, 44 feet

Focal Height: 63 meters, 207 feet

Signal: White flash every 5 seconds

Foghorn Signal: Blast every 20 seconds

Visitor Access: Grounds open, tower closed

Brigus Lighthouse

Due to seal hunting, the Brigus Harbour became a busy harbour in the 1800s. The Brigus Lighthouse opened in 1885 and it initially showed a fixed red light. The light is still active and shows a white flash every 3 seconds. It was listed as a Recognized Federal Heritage Building in 1990.

Description: Cylindrical tower

Location: Brigus

Directions: Strenuous trail from Battery Road in Brigus to the lighthouse or view from Brigus waterfront

Coordinates: 47°32'54.6"N 53°10'55.2"W

Opened: 1885

Automated: 1931

Deactivated: Active

Height: 9 meters, 31 feet

Focal Height: 34 meters, 113 feet

Signal: White flash every 3 seconds

Foghorn signal: N/A

Visitor Access: Grounds open, tower closed

Broad Cove Point Range Front Lighthouse

The original Broad Cove Point Range Front Lighthouse was a wooden tower built in 1918 at Broad Cove Point, on the mainland opposite Long Point, to mark the eastern entrance to Port au Port Bay. In 1955, range lights were built at Broad Cove Point to replace the 1918 tower. In 2005 the lights were deactivated and the rear tower was dismantled. The front tower passed into private hands and was moved to its present location. It can be viewed from the public road.

Description: Square pyramidal wood tower

Location: Point au Mal

Directions: From Point au Mal, head northwest on NL-462 for 4.9 km and the tower can be seen on the right.

Coordinates: 48°41'16.2"N 58°41'00.9"W

Opened: 1955

Automated: 1955

Deactivated: 2005

Height: 9 meters, 31 feet

Focal Height: Not known

Signal: Fixed white

Foghorn Signal: N/A

Visitor Access: Grounds open, tower closed

Burnt Point Lighthouse

The Burnt Point Lighthouse was opened in 1905 when a lantern showing fixed red was shone from the fog alarm building. The site had a keeper's dwelling, a fog alarm building and a store house. The buildings were removed in 1990 and and a square, skeletal tower topped by a metal lantern room replaced the original tower. The signal was changed to a white flash every 6 seconds.

Description: Gray square skeletal tower

Location: Seldom

Directions: From Seldom, head south on Main St for 1.7 km to find the site

Coordinates: 49°36'03.6"N 54°09'29.3"W

Opened: Original 1905, Current 1990

Automated: 1990

Deactivated: Active

Height: 4.5 meters, 15 feet

Focal Height: 16 meters, 62 feet

Signal: White flash every 6 seconds

Foghorn Signal: Blast every 60 seconds

Visitor Access: Grounds open, tower closed

Cabot Islands Lighthouse

Petitions were presented to the Newfoundland Government in 1877 for a lighthouse to be built at the Cabot Islands. In 1880 the Cabot Islands Lighthouse was opened and consisted of a cast iron tower rising from a keeper's dwelling. A 4th order Fresnel lens supplied the lighting. A fog alarm was added to the site in 1921 which was updated in 1950. In 1960 the dwelling was replaced with a smaller building and the tower was covered with reinforced concrete.

Description: Octagonal tower, red and white horizontal bands

Location: Cape Freels

Directions: Accessible by boat

Coordinates: 49°10'28.1"N 53°22'03.3"W

Opened: 1880

Automated: 1954

Deactivated: Active

Height: 15 meters, 50 feet

Focal Height: 22.5 meters, 74 feet

Signal: White flash every 10 seconds

Foghorn Signal: Blast every 60 seconds

Visitor Access: Grounds open, tower closed

Camp Islands Lighthouse

The original Camp Islands Lighthouse was opened on Outer Small Island in 1932 as an aid to ships travelling to Battle Harbour in Labrador. Twillingate Engineering and Construction Ltd. fulfilled a contract for a dwelling, a replacement concrete lighthouse and several smaller buildings in 1960. Camp Islands Light Station was automated in 1996.

Description: White octagonal tower

Location: Lodge Bay

Directions: Accessible by boat

Coordinates: 52°10'02.5"N 55°38'24.8"W

Opened: Original 1931, Current 1961

Automated: 1996

Deactivated: Active

Height: 7 meters, 22 feet

Focal Height: 42 meters, 137 feet

Signal: White flash every 5 seconds

Foghorn signal: New Fog alarm building 1960

Visitor Access: Grounds open, tower closed

Cape Anguille Lighthouse

In 1860 it was noted during a survey by the Engineer for the Province of Canada that a lighthouse was needed to mark the southwest point of Newfoundland. However it was not until 1908 that the original Cape Anguille Lighthouse was built. It had a flying buttress design, one of nine Canadian lighthouses built this way at that time. A fog alarm building was erected at the same time. The tower was lit by a 3rd order Fresnel lens. In 1960 the current tower was built by R. G. McDougall Ltd and it continues to be active.

Description: White, octagonal concrete tower

Location: Shoal Point

Directions: From Shoal Point, head north on NL-406 for 450 meters and turn left on Lighthouse Rd and the site is 1.2 km

Coordinates: 47°54'02.0"N 59°24'40.5"W

Opened: 1960

Automated: 1992

Deactivated: Active

Height: 18 meters, 59 feet

Focal Height: 25 meters, 82 feet

Signal: White flash every 5 seconds

Foghorn signal: Blast every 30 seconds

Visitor Access: Grounds open, tower closed

Cape Bauld Lighthouse

In 1860 the report of a survey proposed Cape Bauld as a proposed location for a lighthouse. The Cape Bauld Lighthouse was completed in 1884 under a contract fulfilled by John A Askwith. The site included a keeper's dwelling and fog alarm building. In 1907 the tower was replaced with one of a flying buttress design. By the 1960s the tower was in poor shape and the present tower opened in 1962 as well as a new keeper's dwelling. It continues to be active.

Description: Hexagonal pyramidal concrete tower

Location: Quirpon

Directions: Accessible by boat

Coordinates: 51°38'24.2"N 55°25'35.9"W

Opened: 1962

Automated: 1996

Deactivated: Active

Height: 15 meters, 50 feet

Focal Height: 54 meters, 177 feet

Signal: White flash every 15 seconds

Foghorn Signal: Blast every 30 seconds

Visitor Access: Grounds open, tower closed

Cape Bonavista Lighthouse

By the 1840s, the Commissioners of Lighthouses proposed a lighthouse be built near Cape Bonavista to guide ships travelling between Bonavista and Trinity Bays. John Saunders fulfilled a contract for the Cape Bonavista Lighthouse and it opened in 1843. A fog alarm was located on nearby Cape Island in 1913. The light was deactivated in 1966 when a skeleton tower was placed nearby. The site has become a popular tourist center which is open in summer.

Description: Cylindrical stone tower

Location: Bonavista

Directions: From Bonavista, head northeast on Cape Shore Rd for 4.2 km and find the site

Coordinates: 48°42'05.2"N 53°05'06.9"W

Opened: Original 1843, Skeleton tower 1966

Automated: 1966

Deactivated: Original 1966, Skeleton Tower Active

Height: 11 meters, 36 feet

Focal Height: 51 meters, 167 feet

Signal: White flash every 10 seconds

Foghorn Signal: Blast every 30 seconds

Visitor Access: Ground open, tower open mid-May to mid-October

Cape Norman Lighthouse

The original Cape Norman Lighthouse opened in 1871 to aid mariners travelling to the eastern entrance at Belle Isle. In 1906 a cylindrical iron tower replaced the original tower with a 3rd order Fresnel lens as lighting. A new fog alarm building and keeper's dwelling were built in 1908 and the tower was encased in concrete and had buttresses added. The current tower opened in 1964 and remains active.

Description: White, octagonal concrete tower

Location: Cape Norman

Directions: From Cape Norman, head north on an unnamed road for 1.8 km and find the site

Coordinates: 51°37'41.7"N 55°54'21.2"W

Opened: 1964

Automated: 1992

Deactivated: Active

Height: 15 meters, 50 feet

Focal Height: 35 meters, 116 feet

Signal: 3 white flashes every 30 seconds

Foghorn signal: Blast every 30 seconds

Visitor Access: Grounds open, tower closed

Cape Pine Lighthouse

In the 1840s the Commissioners of Lighthouses strongly recommended erecting a lighthouse at Cape Pine as it was the site of many shipwrecks. In 1816 the HMS Harpooner struck a reef near Cape Pine and more than 200 passengers drowned. The Cape Pine Lighthouse opened in 1851 when the cast iron curved sections were shipped to the site for installation. A fog alarm was added to the site in 1910. Cape Pine Lighthouse was listed as a National Historic Site in 1974 and a Recognized Federal Heritage Building in 1989.

Description: Cylindrical tower, red and white horizontal bands

Location: St Shott's

Directions: From St Shotts, head NW on St Shotts Rd for 9.2 km and turn right onto Cape Pine Rd and the site is 16.6 km

Coordinates: 46°37'01.1"N 53°31'53.1"W

Opened: 1851

Automated: 1996

Deactivated: Active

Height: 15 meters, 49 feet

Focal Height: 96 meters, 315 feet

Signal: White flash every 5 seconds

Foghorn signal: Blast every 60 seconds

Visitor Access: Grounds open, tower closed

Cape Race Lighthouse

Cape Race is the southeast point of Newfoundland and a very busy shipping area with vessels travelling between Europe and North America. The Cape Race Lighthouse opened in 1852 with the site including a fog alarm, telegraph station, and wireless station. The wireless station famously received the first SOS from the titanic in 1912 and helped coordinate rescue efforts. The tower was covered with curved iron plates which were shipped in from England. In 1907 a new reinforced concrete tower replaced the original. The original was moved to Cape North in Nova Scotia and later to Ottawa at the National Museum of Science and Technology.

Description: White cylindrical tower

Location: Portugal Cove South

Directions: From Cape Race, head SW on an unnamed road for 800 meters and turn left on an unnamed road for 170 meters to find the site

Coordinates: 46°39'30.9"N 53°04'25.0"W

Opened: 1907

Automated: 2012

Deactivated: Active

Height: 29 meters, 96 feet

Focal Height: 52 meters, 170 feet

Signal: White flash every 7.5 seconds

Foghorn Signal: 2 blasts every 60 seconds (discontinued in 1991)

Visitor Access: Grounds open, tower closed

Cape Ray Lighthouse

The original Cape Ray Lighthouse opened in 1871 as an aid to ships travelling to and from Europe through Cabot Strait. In April of 1885, the lighthouse was destroyed by fire. A replacement was quickly completed that same year with the work done by T. Routier. In 1906, a new lantern room and a first-order Fresnel lens were completed. This tower also suffered a fire in 1958. The current tower opened in 1960 and is still active.

Description: White octagonal tower

Location: Cape Ray

Directions: From Cape Ray, head south on Cape Ray/NL-408 for 2.7 km to find the site

Coordinates: 47°37'16.0"N 59°18'14.1"W

Opened: Original 1871, Second 1885, Current 1959

Automated: 1991

Deactivated: Active

Height: 15 meters, 48 feet

Focal Height: 37 meters, 120 feet

Signal: White flash every 15 seconds

Foghorn signal: Blast every 60 seconds

Visitor Access: Grounds open, tower closed

Cape Spear Lighthouse (new)

The easternmost point in North America is Cape Spear which is near the entrance to St. John's Harbour. It was a useful location for a lighthouse and the original light was opened there in 1836. It was deactivated and replaced by the current tower in 1955. This new tower presents a very pleasing appearance against a background of sea and rock. It is still active with a signal of 3 white flashes every 15 seconds.

Description: White hexagonal tower

Location: Black Head

Directions: From Blackhead, head east on Blackhead Rd/NL-11 for 2.9 km to find the site

Coordinates: 47°31'16.2"N 52°37'20.3"W

Opened: 1955

Automated: 1997

Deactivated: Active

Height: 11 meters, 35 feet

Focal Height: 71 meters, 233 feet

Signal: 3 white flashes every 15 seconds

Foghorn Signal: Blast every 60 seconds

Visitor Access: Grounds open, tower closed

Cape Spear Lighthouse (old)

The easternmost point in North America is Cape Spear which is near the entrance to St. John's Harbour. It was a useful location for a lighthouse and the original light was opened there in 1836. This is the oldest surviving lighthouse in Newfoundland. It was deactivated and replaced by the current tower in 1955. It was listed as a National Historic Site in 1962.

Description: Octagonal stone tower projecting from square dwelling

Location: Black Head

Directions: From Blackhead, head east on Blackhead Rd/NL-11 for 2.9 km to find the site

Coordinates: 47°31'11.8"N 52°37'24.0"W

Opened: 1836

Automated: N/A

Deactivated: 1955

Height: 11 meters, 35 feet

Focal Height: N/A

Signal: 3 flashes every 15 seconds

Foghorn Signal: Blast every 60 seconds

Visitor Access: Grounds open, tower open 1st of June through early September

Cape St Francis

The original Cape St Francis Lighthouse opened in 1877 as an aid to ships entering using the southern entrance to Conception Bay. It was built by Cameron and Carnell. Fog control equipment was installed that same year. In 1957, the original Cape St. Francis Lighthouse was replaced with a new keepers' dwelling with a concrete tower that contained the fog signal equipment and was topped by a light. It continues to be active.

Description: Octagonal lantern house on rectangular building

Location: Pouch Cove

Directions: From Pouch Cove, head NW on Main Rd/NL-20 N for 4.6 km to find the site

Coordinates: 47°48'31.4"N 52°47'11.7"W

Opened: Original 1877, current 1957

Automated: 1975

Deactivated: Active

Height: 3.3 meters, 11 feet

Focal Height: 29 meters, 95 feet

Signal: White flash every 5 seconds

Foghorn Signal: Fog alarm attached to dwelling

Visitor Access: Grounds open, tower closed

Cape St. Mary's Lighthouse

The Cape St. Mary's Lighthouse was built at the southwestern tip of the Avalon Peninsula in 1860 as an aid to the fisheries in the area. It is by the Cape St. Mary's Ecological Reserve which was established in 1983 for one of the largest seabird colonies. The brick tower has been greatly modified over the years. It was coated with cement in 1869, by cast iron in 1886, and in the 1950s encased in concrete. It was listed as a a Recognized Federal Heritage Building in 2007 and is still active.

Description: White octagonal tower

Location: St Bride's

Directions: From St Bride's, head SW on The Cape Shore Hwy/NL-100 S for 4.0 km and turn right on an unnamed road for 12.8 km and find the site

Coordinates: 46°49'23.0"N 54°11'45.6"W

Opened: 1860

Automated: 1994

Deactivated: Active

Height: 17 meters, 55 feet

Focal Height: 96 meters, 314 feet

Signal: White flash every 5 seconds

Foghorn Signal: Blast every 30 seconds

Visitor Access: Grounds open, tower closed

Channel Head Lighthouse

The Channel Head Lighthouse opened in 1875 as an aid to ships travelling off Port aux Basques. It showed a fixed red light at that time. It was replaced by a circular iron tower in 1895 and equipped with a 4th order lens. In 1906, a diaphone fog alarm upgraded the equipment. The tower was listed as a Recognized Federal Heritage Building in 1988 and continues to be active.

Description: White cylindrical tower

Location: Channel-Port aux Basques

Directions: Accessible by boat, viewable from the waterfront in Port aux Basques

Coordinates: 47°33'57.0"N 59°07'24.6"W

Opened: 1860

Automated: 1938

Deactivated: Active

Height: 11 meters, 36 feet

Focal Height: 29 meters, 95 feet

Signal: White flash every 10 seconds

Foghorn Signal: Blast every 60 seconds

Visitor Access: Grounds open, tower closed

Cow Head Lighthouse

The Cow Head Lighthouse is situated on the west coast of the Great Northern Peninsula. It opened in 1909. After being deactivated in 1988, it was neglected for years as the image shows. However it had a restoration in 2002 and was repainted in 2019.

Description: Cylindrical mast

Location: Cow Head

Directions: From Cow Head, head SW on Main St for 1.6 km and turn right onto Pond Rd. After 1.2 km, park and take the Cows Head Lighthouse Trail to the site

Coordinates: 49°55'09.8"N 57°49'26.3"W

Opened: 1909

Automated: 1952

Deactivated: 1988

Height: 5 meters, 18 feet

Focal Height: 43 meters, 141 feet

Signal: Fixed white

Foghorn signal: N/A

Visitor Access: Open

Dawson's Point Lighthouse

The original Dawson's Point Lighthouse was a wooden structure that was opened in 1916. It was equipped with a Sun Valve which allowed the site to be automated. It was replaced by a square skeletal tower which is still active.

Description: Square skeleton tower

Location: Pushthrough

Directions: Accessible by boat

Coordinates: 47°38'35.9"N 56°08'57.5"W

Opened: Original 1916, Current not known

Automated: 1916

Deactivated: Active

Height: 4 meters, 13 feet

Focal Height: 17 meters, 56 feet

Signal: White flash every 5 seconds

Foghorn Signal: Blast every 20 seconds

Visitor Access: Grounds open, tower closed

Double Island Lighthouse

The Double Island Lighthouse was erected by the Newfoundland Government in 1905 primarily as an aid to the fishing vessels travelling through the area. The light was automated in 1932 and continues to be active.

Description: Round cylindrical cast iron tower

Location: Lodge Bay

Directions: Accessible by boat

Coordinates: 52°15'18.5"N 55°33'17.0"W

Opened: 1905

Automated: 1932

Deactivated: Active

Height: 7 meters, 23 feet

Focal Height: 38 meters, 126 feet

Signal: White flash every 4 seconds

Foghorn signal: N/A

Visitor Access: Grounds open, tower closed

English Harbour West Lighthouse

In 1921, the English Harbour West Lighthouse was erected on the eastern side of the entrance to English Harbour West. It was deactivated in the 1990s.

Description: Square pyramidal wooden tower

Location: English Harbour West

Directions: From Saint Jacques-Coomb's Cove, head SW on Ocean Dr for 1.6 km to find the site

Coordinates: 47°27'18.0"N 55°29'33.0"W

Opened: 1921

Automated: 1921

Deactivated: Deactivated 1990s, Current Mast Active

Height: 4.5 meters, 15 feet

Focal Height: 14 meters, 45 feet

Signal: Red flash every 4 seconds

Foghorn signal: N/A

Visitor Access: Grounds open, tower closed

Ferryland Head Lighthouse

The Ferryland Head Lighthouse opened in 1871 as an aid to ships approaching the Ferryland Harbour. William Campbell and Thomas Burridge built the tower and the keeper's dwelling. The tower was equipped with a 3rd order Fresnel lens which displayed a fixed white flash. As the brickwork constantly cracked, it was replaced with iron casing in 1892. Ferryland Head Lighthouse was listed as a Recognized Federal Heritage Building in 1991 and is still active.

Description: Red and white cylindrical tower

Location: Ferryland

Directions: From Ferryland, head southeast on The Down's for 180 meters and turn right on an unnamed road for 2.1 km to find the site

Coordinates: 47°01'00.4"N 52°51'26.7"W

Opened: 1871

Automated: 1970

Deactivated: Active

Height: 14 meters, 46 feet

Focal Height: 58 meters, 190 feet

Signal: White flash every 6 seconds

Foghorn Signal: N/A

Visitor Access: Grounds open, dwelling open mid June through September, tower closed

Flowers Cove Lighthouse

The Flowers Cove Lighthouse opened in 1899 as an aid to vessels travelling Newfoundland's west coast. It was built by the Canadian Government who were primarily interested in it's necessity. The work was completed by Canada's Department of Marine. A fog signal was added in 1912. The station was deactivated in 1969.

Description: Square cylindrical wood tower

Location: Flower's Cove

Directions: Accessible only by boat, viewable from Nameless Point, the NW point of the town of Flowers Cove

Coordinates: 51°18'30.1"N 56°44'55.2"W

Opened: 1899

Automated: 1969

Deactivated: 1969

Height: 15.5 meters, 51 feet

Focal Height: Not known

Signal: Green flash every 3 seconds

Foghorn Signal: Fog signal 1912

Visitor Access: Grounds open, tower closed

Fort Amherst Lighthouse

The original Fort Amherst Lighthouse became Newfoundland's first lighthouse when it opened in 1813 to aid ships travelling to St. John Harbour. A replacement tower built by Kerr and Moody was opened in 1853 as the original was in poor shape. After Newfoundland joined Canada, the current lighthouse was built in 1951 and it continues to be active.

Description: White, square pyramidal wooden tower

Location: St. John

Directions: From St. John, head NW on Southside Rd off PE-2 for 1.9 km and continue onto Fort Amherst Rd where the site is 1.0 km

Coordinates: 47°33'47.9"N 52°40'49.6"W

Opened: Original 1813, Second 1852, Current 1951

Automated: 1982

Deactivated: Active

Height: 8 meters, 25 feet

Focal Height: 40 meters, 132 feet

Signal: White flash every 15 seconds

Foghorn Signal: Blast every 20 seconds

Visitor Access: Grounds open, tower closed

Fort Point (Trinity) Lighthouse

Trinity Harbour is one of the largest and finest in Newfoundland and the Fort Point Lighthouse was opened in 1874 to aid ships in the area. In 1908, the light signal was changed from fixed white to an occulting white light. A fog alarm building was added in 1910. A cast iron lighthouse replaced the original in 1921. The iron tower atop was demolished in 1971. and a red skeleton tower replaced it.

Description: White square pyramidal tower

Location: Admiral's Point

Directions: From Coleman's Point, head north on an unnamed road for 1.7 km. and find the site.

Coordinates: 48°21'55.0"N 53°20'42.0"W

Opened: Original 1874, Current 2003

Automated: 2003

Deactivated: Active

Height: 8 meters, 26 feet

Focal Height: 34 meters, 79 feet

Signal: White flash every 5 seconds

Foghorn Signal: 2 blasts every 105 seconds

Visitor Access: Grounds open, tower closed

Fortune Head Lighthouse

The Fortune Harbour was dredged in 1906 to improve it. The Fortune Head Lighthouse was built in 1954 as well as a fog alarm station. Keepers felt the isolation but a road was built to the site in 1968. The station was automated in 1990 and continues to be active.

Description: White pyramidal tower

Location: Fortune

Directions: From Fortune, head south on Eldon St/NL-220 for 1.8 km and turn right onto Hornhouse Rd and find the site in 3.4 km

Coordinates: 47°04'27.7"N 55°51'33.2"W

Opened: Original 1911, Current 1955

Automated: 1990

Deactivated: Active

Height: 9 meters, 30 feet

Focal Height: 24 meters, 79 feet

Signal: White flash every 5 seconds

Foghorn Signal: Blast every 30 seconds

Visitor Access: Grounds open, tower closed

Fox Point (Fishing Point) Lighthouse

Fox Point designates the eastern side of the entrance to St. Anthony Harbour. In 1912 a circular iron lighthouse was built at Fox Point. A fog alarm building was added to the site in 1936. In 1960 it was replaced with a single story building with a square tower. A skeletal tower provides an active signal today.

Description: White pyramidal tower

Location: Fishing Point

Directions: From Pateyville, head east on Fishing Point Rd for 1.0 km to find the site.

Coordinates: 51°21'22.0"N 55°33'18.3"W

Opened: Original 1912, Current 2003

Automated: 2003

Deactivated: Active

Height: 6 meters, 26 feet

Focal Height: 27 meters, 88 feet

Signal: White flash every 10 seconds

Foghorn signal: Blast every 60 seconds

Visitor Access: Grounds open, tower closed

François Bay (West Point) Lighthouse

François Bay is a deep fjord on the south coast of Newfoundland. A fog alarm station was built on West Point in 1929. The François Bay (West Point) Lighthouse was erected in 1958 on West Point. In 1966 it was replaced by a new lighthouse and fog alarm building. The lighthouse was listed as a Recognized Federal Heritage Building in 2007.

Description: White square tower

Location: François

Directions: Accessible by boat

Coordinates: 47°33'35.7"N 56°44'02.1"W

Opened: Original 1958, Current 1966

Automated: 1966

Deactivated: Active

Height: 14 meters, 46 feet

Focal Height: 46 meters, 151 feet

Signal: Green flash every 5 seconds

Foghorn Signal: Blast every 60 seconds

Visitor Access: Grounds open, tower closed

Garnish Lighthouse

Granish is located on the west coast of the Burin Peninsula and has a small harbour. The original lighthouse was built in 1877 and relocated to the breakwater. The deactivated historic lighthouse was removed from the breakwater in the last 1930s or early 1940s and has since been renovated by the Garnish Heritage Society. The light is now sent from a square skeletal tower.

Description: White square pyramidal tower

Location: Garnish

Directions: From Garnish, head east on Seaview Dr for a short distance to the site.

Coordinates: 47°14'10.2"N 55°21'30.6"W

Opened: 1885

Automated: 1967

Deactivated: Active

Height: 6 meters, 20 feet

Focal Height: 8 meters, 28 feet

Signal: Red flash every 3 seconds

Foghorn signal: N/A

Visitor Access: Grounds open, tower closed

Grand Bank Wharf Lighthouse

The original Grand Bank Wharf Light was a wooden tower displaying a fixed white light opened in 1890. The current octagonal concrete tower was erected in 1922 on the eastern pier at Grand Bank harbour. It continues to be active.

Description: White, square pyramidal concrete tower

Location: Grand Bank

Directions: In Grand Bank, head north on Fishplant Road off Marine Dr to find the site.

Coordinates: 47°06'04.7"N 55°44'57.8"W

Opened: 1920

Automated: 1950s

Deactivated: Active

Height: 7 meters, 23 feet

Focal Height: 8 meters, 27 feet

Signal: White flash every 4 seconds

Foghorn Signal: N/A

Visitor Access: Grounds open, tower closed

Green Island Light (Catalina)

The Green Island Lighthouse was opened in 1857 as an aid to ships entering Catalina Harbour. The construction contract was completed by Alexander Smith. In 1882 a fog control building was added to the site and in 1909 it was upgraded. In 1956 the dwelling was removed and the tower was covered in concrete. The tower was listed as a Recognized Federal Heritage Building in 1990.

Description: Red and white octagonal tower

Location: Catalina

Directions: Accessible by boat

Coordinates: 48°30'14.9"N 53°02'35.8"W

Opened: 1857

Automated: Still staffed

Deactivated: Active

Height: 9 meters, 30 feet

Focal Height: 238 meters, 92 feet

Signal: 3 white flashes every 12 seconds

Foghorn signal: Blast every 60 seconds

Visitor Access: Grounds open, tower closed

Green Point Lighthouse

Green Point or Bay Roberts Point is at the eastern end of the Port de Grave Peninsula, which delineates the southern side of the entrance to Bay Roberts Harbour. The Green Point Lighthouse was erected in 1883 to aid ships travelling to that destination. The tower was listed as a Recognized Federal Heritage Building in 1990.

Description: Cylindrical tower, red and white horizontal bands

Location: Port de Grave

Directions: There is a rough gravel road from Hibb's Cove that leads to the lighthouse, about 2 km

Coordinates: 47°36'41.4"N 53°10'36.1"W

Opened: 1883

Automated: 1930s

Deactivated: Active

Height: 9 meters, 30 feet

Focal Height: 17 meters, 56 feet

Signal: White flash every 10 seconds

Foghorn signal: N/A

Visitor Access: Grounds open, tower closed

Gull Island (Cape St. John) Lighthouse

In 1867 the ship Queen of Swansea wrecked on Gull Island in a gale and all aboard perished. This prompted the building of the Gull Island (Cape St. John) Lighthouse, although it didn't open until 1884. A fog alarm building with a keeper's dwelling was added in 1916. The tower was listed as a Recognized Federal Heritage Building in 1989. The light was moved to a skeletal tower in 2014 when the old tower was deactivated.

Description: Square skeleton tower

Location: Shoe Cove

Directions: Accessible by boat

Coordinates: 49°59'48.3"N 55°21'54.4"W

Opened: Original 1884, Current 2014

Automated: 2014

Deactivated: Active

Height: 11.5 meters, 38 feet

Focal Height: 160 meters, 525 feet

Signal: White flash every 10 seconds

Foghorn Signal: Blast every 30 seconds

Visitor Access: Closed

Hant's Harbour Lighthouse

The Newfoundland House of Assembly budgeted funds for the original Hant's Harbour Lighthouse which opened in 1881 to aid ships entering Hant's Harbour. In 1893 the lighting was upgraded to a 6th order lens. The current tower was opened in 1957. The site has had parking and picnic tables made available for visitors.

Description: Square pyramidal wood tower

Location: Hant's Harbour

Directions: From Hant's Harbour, head NW on Custers Head Rd for 850 meters and the lighthouse is a short walk

Coordinates: 48°01'18.5"N 53°15'15.8"W

Opened: Original 1881, Current 1957

Automated: 1957

Deactivated: Active

Height: 9 meters, 30 feet

Focal Height: 20 meters, 65 feet

Signal: White flash every 6 seconds

Foghorn signal: N/A

Visitor Access: Grounds open, tower closed

Harbour Point (Sandy Point) Lighthouse

Sandy Point or Harbour Point was at the tip of a peninsula into St. George's Bay which was cut by a gale in 1951 and is now Flat Island. The Harbour Point (Sandy Point) Lighthouse was the first lighthouse on the west coast of Newfoundland when erected in 1883. It was restored in 1989 and again in 2010. The Sandy Point name is used locally.

Description: Cylindrical tower, red and white horizontal bands

Location: Saint George's

Directions: Accessible by boat

Coordinates: 48°27'26.2"N 58°29'19.7"W

Opened: 1883

Automated: 1967

Deactivated: Active

Height: 9 meters, 31 feet

Focal Height: 11 meters, 35 feet

Signal: White flash every 6 seconds

Foghorn Signal: N/A

Visitor Access: Grounds open, tower closed

Heart's Content Lighthouse

An 1893 survey for lighthouse locations identified Heart's Content as an appropriate site. In 1901 the Heart's Content Lighthouse was opened at Norther Point. The lighthouse was listed as a Recognized Federal Heritage Building in 1990 and continues to be active.

Description: Red and white cylindrical tower

Location: Heart's Content

Directions: From Heart's Content, head north on Trinity Rd S/Trinity Rd South 80/NL-80 for 450 meters and take a slight left onto N Point Rd and the site is 1.2 km

Coordinates: 47°52'55.9"N 53°23'06.4"W

Opened: 1901

Automated: 1931

Deactivated: Active

Height: 9 meters, 30 feet

Focal Height: 25 meters, 83 feet

Signal: White flash every 6 seconds

Foghorn signal: N/A

Visitor Access: Grounds open, tower closed

Keppel Island Lighthouse

The Keppel Island Lighthouse was opened in 1901 as an aid to ships travelling the southern side of the entrance to Port Saunders and the northern side of the entrance to Hawke's Bay. In 1957, a keeper's dwelling, a fog alarm building and 2 storage buildings were added to the site. The light was deactivated in 1992 and a skeletal tower replaced it.

Description: Square, pyramidal wooden tower

Location: Port Saunders

Directions: Accessible by boat

Coordinates: 50°37'58.9"N 57°19'19.9"W

Opened: 1901

Automated: 1989

Deactivated: 1992

Height: 11 meters, 37 feet

Focal Height: 37 meters, 121 feet

Signal: White flash every 16 seconds

Foghorn signal: Blast every 30 seconds

Visitor Access: Grounds open, tower closed

Kings Cove Head Lighthouse

A petition from residents of King's Cove for a lighthouse at King's Cove's Western Point was sent to the Newfoundland government in 1873. However it was not until 1893 before the Kings Cove Head Lighthouse was opened. Cast iron sections for the tower were manufactured in England and shipped to the site. The tower was painted white in 1897 to make it more visible against the treed background. It was listed as a Recognized Federal Heritage Building in 1990.

Description: White, conical cast iron tower

Location: King's Cove

Directions: From King's Cove, head east on Top Rd for 350 meters and turn right onto Chapel Hl. After 200 meters, take trail for 500 meters to the site.

Coordinates: 48°34'32.0"N 53°19'25.0"W

Opened: 1893

Automated: 1992

Deactivated: Active

Height: 11 meters, 36 feet

Focal Height: 54 meters, 176 feet

Signal: White flash every 4 seconds

Foghorn : Fog horn active from 1930-1940

Visitor Access: Grounds open, tower closed

Little Denier Island Lighthouse

The Little Denier Island Lighthouse was built in 1888 for ships travelling to Bonavista Bay. Mr. Cornick built the tower and the site was completed in 14 weeks. The tower was listed as a Recognized Federal Heritage Building in 1990. and continues to be active.

Description: Round cylindrical cast iron tower

Location: Salvage

Directions: Accessible by boat

Coordinates: 48°41'05.0"N 53°34'24.0"W

Opened: 1888

Automated: 1960s

Deactivated: Active

Height: 9 meters, 30 feet

Focal Height: 91 meters, 298 feet

Signal: White flash every 3 seconds

Foghorn Signal: N/A

Visitor Access: Closed

Lobster Cove Head Lighthouse

The Lobster Cove Head Lighthouse was erected in 1897 to aid ships travelling to Boone Bay. The iron tower was made by Victoria Iron Works of St. John's. Lobster Cove Head Lighthouse was listed as a Recognized Federal Heritage Building in 1990. It was automated 1970 and continues to be active.

Description: White, conical cast iron tower

Location: Lobster Cove

Directions: From Rocky Harbour, head NW on Main St N/Hwy 15 for 2.6 km and turn left on an unnamed road and the site is 450 meters

Coordinates: 49°36'10.3"N 57°57'21.3"W

Opened: 1897

Automated: 1970

Deactivated: Active

Height: 8 meters, 28 feet

Focal Height: 35 meters, 115 feet

Signal: White flash every 4 seconds

Foghorn Signal: N/A

Visitor Access: Grounds open, tower closed

Long Point (Twillingate) Lighthouse

The Long Point (Twillingate) Lighthouse was opened in 1876 to mark the entrance to Twillingate Harbour. The contractors were Messrs. Colman and Kelly. In 1920 a fog alarm building was added to the site. After a 1929 earthquake caused cracking in the tower's bricks, it was enclosed in reinforced concrete. The lighthouse and double dwelling were listed as Recognized Federal Heritage Buildings in 1989 and the site continues to be active.

Description: Red and white rectangular tower

Location: Crow Head

Directions: From Crow Head, head NW on Lighthouse Rd/Main St/NL-340 N and continue to follow Lighthouse Rd/NL-340 N for 1.4 km and find the light

Coordinates: 49°41'16.0"N 54°48'00.0"W

Opened: 1876

Automated: Still staffed

Deactivated: Active

Height: 15 meters, 50 feet

Focal Height: 202 meters, 331 feet

Signal: White flash every 5 seconds

Foghorn Signal: Blast every 60 seconds

Visitor Access: Grounds open, tower open on occasion

Manuel Island Lighthouse

The Manuel Island Lighthouse was erected at the entrance of Catalina Harbour on Manuel Island in 1916. The light is accessible only by boat but can be viewed from the waterfront of Catalina Harbour, south of Bonavista.

Description: Round cylindrical cast iron tower

Location: Catalina

Directions: Accessible by boat, viewable from Courage's Point in Catalina Harbour

Coordinates: 48°30'40.4"N 53°04'02.2"W

Opened: 1918

Automated: 1963

Deactivated: Not known

Height: 5 meters, 16 feet

Focal Height: 8 meters, 26 feet

Signal: Fixed red

Foghorn signal: N/A

Visitor Access: Grounds open, tower closed

Middle Head Lighthouse

In 1912, A fog alarm was opened on Middle Head which is situated by Great and Little St. Lawrence Harbours and in 1915 a light was added to the site. The site was destroyed in a fire in 1919. The lighthouse and fog control building were rebuilt in 1920. The signal is currently sent from a square skeleton tower built in 1991, The keeper's dwelling has been removed.

Description: Square skeleton tower

Location: St. Lawrence

Directions: From St. Lawrence, head SW on Water St E for 800 m and turn left onto Lighthouse Rd where the site is 3.4 km

Coordinates: 46°53'52.8"N 55°20'51.2"W

Opened: 1915

Automated: 1968

Deactivated: Active

Height: 9.5 meters, 31 feet

Focal Height: 27 meters, 89 feet

Signal: White flash every 15 seconds

Foghorn Signal: Blast every 30 seconds

Visitor Access: Grounds open, tower closed

New Férolle Peninsula Lighthouse

The New Férolle Peninsula Lighthouse was erected in 1913 on Point Ferolle as protection for ships travelling the Gulf of St Lawrence. The site included a fog alarm building, a dwelling for the keepers, an oil house, and a boathouse along with the concrete tower with 6 buttresses. The lighting equipment included a 3rd order Fresnel lens. A new fog alarm building was built in 1976. The site continues to be active.

Description: White, hexagonal reinforced concrete tower

Location: New Ferolle

Directions: From New Ferolle, head NW on an unnamed road for 300 meters and turn left on an unnamed road and the site is 2.7 km

Coordinates: 51°01'22.1"N 57°05'44.5"W

Opened: 1913

Automated: Still staffed

Deactivated: Active

Height: 19 meters, 64 feet

Focal Height: 27 meters, 91 feet

Signal: 4 white flashes every 7.5 seconds

Foghorn signal: 3 blasts every 60 seconds

Visitor Access: Grounds open, tower closed

Northwest Head (Ramea) Lighthouse

The Northwest Head Lighthouse was opened in 1902 as an aid to the local fisheries. A diaphone foghorn was added to the site in 1952. The lighthouse continues to be active.

Description: White cylindrical tower

Location: Ramea

Directions: From Ramea, head SW on Valley Rd for 300 meters and turn left onto Muddyhole Rd. After 400 meters, park and take trail to site (700 meters)

Coordinates: 47°30'44.9"N 57°24'31.5"W

Opened: 1902

Automated: 1970

Deactivated: Active

Height: 9 meters, 30 feet

Focal Height: 38 meters, 125 feet

Signal: White flash every 3 seconds

Foghorn Signal: Blast every 30 seconds

Visitor Access: Grounds open, tower closed

Offer Wadham Island Lighthouse

In 1841 requests were made to the Governor of Newfoundland for a lighthouse on the Wadham Islands, a group of islands off the northeast point of Newfoundland. Funds were finally made available and William Campbell fulfilled the contract and the light opened in 1858. The brick tower was encased in concrete in 1863. A 3th order Fresnel lens was installed in 1890. The light currently is sent from a skeletal tower while the old tower still survives.

Description: Octagonal concrete tower, lantern removed

Location: Musgrave Harbour

Directions: Accessible by boat

Coordinates: 49°35'36.3"N 53°45'46.1"W

Opened: Original 1858, Steel skeletal tower early 1990s

Automated: 1966

Deactivated: Early 1990s

Height: 12 meters, 40 feet

Focal Height: 30.5 meters, 100 feet

Signal: White flash every 3 seconds

Foghorn signal: N/A

Visitor Access: Grounds open, tower closed

Peckford Island Lighthouse

The Peckford Island Lighthouse was built in 1910 to aid ships moving into Hamilton Sound. A fog alarm was added to the site in 1926. In 1961, Davis Construction Ltd erected the current skeleton tower and a fog alarm building while the other buildings were demolished.

Description: Square brick tower attached to fog signal building

Location: Musgrave Harbour

Directions: Accessible by boat

Coordinates: 49°31'49.6"N 53°51'04.8"W

Opened: Original 1910 (Image above), Current 1961

Automated: 1995

Deactivated: Original 1961, Current skeleton tower active

Height: 7 meters, 24 feet

Focal Height: 16 meters, 61 feet

Signal: White flash every 10 seconds

Foghorn Signal: Blast every 30 seconds

Visitor Access: Grounds open, tower closed

Point Amour Lighthouse

The Point Amour Lighthouse is the tallest lighthouse in Newfoundland and the second tallest in Canada. It was erected in 1858 to aid mariners travelling through the Strait of Belle Isle. The tower was equipped with a 2nd order Fresnel lens. In 1878, a steam whistle originally from Cape Ray was installed at the site. The lighthouse was listed as a Classified Federal Heritage Building in 1987.

Description: Limestone covered with brick and clapboard tower

Location: L'Anse-Amour

Directions: From L'Anse-Amour, head SW on L'Anse Amour Branch Rd for 1.6 km and turn right where the site is 250 meters

Coordinates: 51°27'37.7"N 56°51'29.3"W

Opened: 1858

Automated: 1960s

Deactivated: Active

Height: 33 meters, 109 feet

Focal Height: 46 meters, 152 feet

Signal: White flash every 20 seconds

Foghorn Signal: Blast every 30 seconds

Visitor Access: Grounds open, tower open mid-May to early October

Point Riche Lighthouse

The first Point Riche Lighthouse was opened by the Canadian government in 1871 to assist steamers passing through the Strait of Belle Isle on trips between the St. Lawrence and Europe. A Neptune foghorn was added to the site in 1877. The lighthouse was destroyed by fire in 1890. The current lighthouse was opened in 1892 after being built by Daniel McDonald. In 1908 a 3rd order Fresnel lens upgraded the lighting equipment. Pointe Riche Lighthouse was listed as a Recognized Federal Heritage Building in 1991.

Description: Octagonal tower

Location: Port au Choix

Directions: From Port au Choix, head southwest on Point Riche Rd for 3.7 km to find the site

Coordinates: 50°41'54.6"N 57°24'36.8"W

Opened: 1892

Automated: 1970

Deactivated: Active

Height: 19 meters, 63 feet

Focal Height: 39 meters, 96 feet

Signal: White flash every 5 seconds

Foghorn signal: Blast every 10 minutes

Visitor Access: Grounds open, tower closed

Point Verde Lighthouse

The original Point Verde Lighthouse opened in 1879 as protection against reefs northwest of Point Verde. A fog alarm was added to the site in 1912. The current tower was erected in 1990 and is the 5th tower at the site. It continues to be active.

Description: Square skeleton tower

Location: Point Verde

Directions: From Point Verde, head NW on an unnamed road for 1.3 km and find the site

Coordinates: 47°14'15.0"N 54°00'55.0"W

Opened: Original 1879, Current 1990

Automated: 1990

Deactivated: Active

Height: 11 meters, 37 feet

Focal Height: 30 meters, 98 feet

Signal: White flash every 5 seconds

Foghorn signal: Blast every 60 seconds

Visitor Access: Closed

Powles Head Lighthouse

The original Powles Head Lighthouse was a square, pyramidal wooden tower joined to a keeper's dwelling by a passageway. It was erected in 1902 and equipped with a 5th order lens. In 1907 the fog alarm was upgraded to a diaphone. The current tower opened in 1960 and continues to be active.

Description: Square, white wooden tower with red lantern

Location: Trepassey

Directions: From Trepassey, head SW on Battery Rd/Lower Rd for 1.1 km to reach the site.

Coordinates: 46°41'25.1"N 53°24'05.7"W

Opened: Original 1902, Current 1960

Automated: 1960

Deactivated: Active

Height: 9 meters, 30 feet

Focal Height: 31 meters, 101 feet

Signal: White flash every 10 seconds

Foghorn Signal: Blast every 30 seconds

Visitor Access: Grounds open, tower closed

Puffin Island Lighthouse

The original Puffin Island Lighthouse opened in 1873 as an aid to ships entering Greenspond Harbour. Smith and Haw used granite blocks quarried nearby to build the tower and attached keeper's dwelling. A diaphone fog alarm was added to the station in 1914. A square wooden tower replaced the original in 1951.

Description: Red and white hexagonal tower

Location: Greenspond

Directions: Accessible by boat, viewable from Greenspond waterfront

Coordinates: 49°03'42.2"N 53°33'06.9"W

Opened: 1951

Automated: Still staffed

Deactivated: Active

Height: 8 meters, 25 feet

Focal Height: 21 meters, 70 feet

Signal: White flash every 5 seconds

Foghorn Signal: Blast every 30 seconds

Visitor Access: Grounds open, tower closed

Random Head Harbour Lighthouse

The Random Head Harbour Lighthouse was erected in 1895 to aid ships navigating the Random Island perimeter. Random Island became joined to the mainland by a causeway built in 1952. A 6th order lens equipped the tower lighting. The tower was listed as a Recognized Federal Heritage Building in 1990.

Description: Red and white cylindrical tower

Location: Hickman's Harbour

Directions: Accessible by boat

Coordinates: 48°05'41.1"N 53°32'43.1"W

Opened: 1895

Automated: 1960s

Deactivated: Active

Height: 10 meters, 34 feet

Focal Height: 38 meters, 126 feet

Signal: Red flash every 3 seconds

Foghorn signal: N/A

Visitor Access: Closed

Rocky Point (Harbour Breton) Lighthouse

The quick red fox jumped over the lazy brown dog. The quick red fox jumped over the lazy brown dog. The quick red fox jumped over the lazy brown dog. The quick red fox jumped over the lazy brown dog. The quick red fox jumped over the lazy brown dog. The quick red fox jumped over the lazy brown dog. The quick red fox jumped over the lazy brown dog. The quick red fox jumped over the lazy brown dog. The quick red fox jumped over the lazy brown dog. The quick red fox jumped over the lazy brown dog. The quick red fox jumped over the lazy brown dog. The quick red fox jumped over the lazy brown dog. The quick red fox jumped over the lazy brown dog. The quick red fox jumped over the lazy brown dog.

Description: Red and white cylindrical tower

Location: Harbour Breton

Directions: From Harbour Breton, head NW on Bay d'Espoir Hwy S for 2.1 km and take a slight left onto Rocky Pt Rd where the site is 400 meters

Coordinates: 47°28'46.3"N 55°47'34.4"W

Opened: 1881

Automated: 1931

Deactivated: Active

Height: 7.5 meters, 25 feet

Focal Height: 16 meters, 52 feet

Signal: White flash every 4 seconds

Foghorn signal: N/A

Visitor Access: Grounds open, tower closed

Rose Blanche Lighthouse

In 1873, the Rose Blanche Lighthouse was built on the eastern head at the Rose Blanche harbour entrance using granite quarried nearby. Smith and Haw acted as contractors for the 12 meter tower. In 1891 the southern and eastern sides of the tower received red and white vertical stripes to make the lighthouse more visible. The tower collapsed in 1957, but was reconstructed in 1996 after it was recognized as a potential tourist attraction. The lighthouse became the first in Newfoundland to be listed as a Registered Heritage Structure

Description: Octagonal granite light tower

Location: Rose Blanche

Directions: From Rose Blanche-Harbour le Cou, head southeast on Big Bottom Rd for 260 meters and turn left onto Water Bottom Rd. After 1.3 km you will find the site

Coordinates: 47°36'06.7"N 58°41'40.9"W

Opened: Original 1873, Current 1996

Automated: 1996

Deactivated: Active

Height: 12 meters, 40 feet

Focal Height: 29 meters, 95 feet

Signal: Red flash every 10 seconds

Foghorn Signal: Blast every 60 seconds

Visitor Access: Grounds open, tower open mid-May through October

St. Jacques Island Lighthouse

The St. Jacques Island Lighthouse was built in 1908 to protect ships entering St. Jacques Harbour. The lighting equipment was a 4th order Fresnel lens. A fog alarm was added to the site in 1929. The lighthouse was listed as a Recognized Federal Heritage Building in 1989.

Description: White cylindrical tower

Location: St. Jacques

Directions: Accessible by boat

Coordinates: 47°28'26.0"N 55°24'23.0"W

Opened: 1908

Automated: 1963

Deactivated: Active

Height: 9 meters, 40 feet

Focal Height: 40 meters, 131 feet

Signal: White flash every 6 seconds

Foghorn Signal: Blast every 30 seconds

Visitor Access: Grounds open, tower closed

St. Modeste Island Lighthouse

The original St. Modeste Island Lighthouse opened about 1920 for ships entering a channel known as The Tickle near West St. Modeste. The present wooden, pyramidal tower was built in 1956.

Description: Square pyramidal wooden tower

Location: West St. Modeste

Directions: Accessible by boat

Coordinates: 51°35'43.0"N 56°42'02.0"W

Opened: 1956

Automated: 1963

Deactivated: 2010

Height: 5.5 meters, 18 feet

Focal Height: Not known

Signal: Red flash every 3 seconds

Foghorn signal: Blast every 20 seconds

Visitor Access: Grounds open, tower closed

Tides Cove Point Lighthouse

A fog alarm was established at Tide's Point in 1912 and in 1915 the original Tides Cove Point Lighthouse was added to the site. In 1957 S.J. Scott built a lighthouse and fog alarm building to replace the originals. In 1992 the current square skeleton tower was built and the site was automated. However it was re-staffed in 2003.

Description: Square skeleton tower

Location: Fox Cove

Directions: From Fox Cove-Mortier, head east on an unnamed road off NF-221 for 3.5 km to find the site

Coordinates: 47°06'21.7"N 55°04'20.9"W

Opened: Original 1915, Current 1993

Automated: Restaffed in 2003

Deactivated: Active

Height: 9.5 meters, 31 feet

Focal Height: 33.5 meters, 110 feet

Signal: White flash every 6 seconds

Foghorn signal: Blast every 60 seconds

Visitor Access: Grounds open, tower closed

Westport Cove Lighthouse

The Westport Cove Lighthouse was built in 1911 as an aid to fishermen and other coastal ships. The site was automated in 1989 and remains active today. This may be Canada's smallest lighthouse.

Description: White octagonal tower

Location: Westport

Directions: From Westport, head NW on an unnamed road from Ocean View Road for 200 meters and take the trail for 200 meters to the site

Coordinates: 49°47'10.9"N 56°38'45.2"W

Opened: 1911

Automated: 1989

Deactivated: Active

Height: 5.5 meters, 18 feet

Focal Height: 10 meters, 33 feet

Signal: White flash every 4 seconds

Foghorn signal: N/A

Visitor Access: Grounds open, tower closed

Woody Point Lighthouse

The original Woody Point Lighthouse was a square, pyramidal, wooden tower built in 1919 as an aid to ships travelling to the entrance to Bonnie Bay. The current tower replaced it in 1959 when it was automated. The lighthouse was listed with a Federal Heritage designation in 2016.

Description: White, square pyramidal wooden tower

Location: Bonnie Bay

Directions: 61 Water St, Woody Point

Coordinates: 49°30'17.5"N 57°54'46.4"W

Opened: Original 1919, Current 1959

Automated: 1959

Deactivated: Active

Height: 6 meters, 20 feet

Focal Height: 14 meters, 45 feet

Signal: Red flash every 4 seconds

Foghorn signal: N/A

Visitor Access: Grounds open, tower closed

Other Lighthouses

Name: Baccalieu Island southwest point
Opened: 1953
Coordinates: 48°06'24.3"N 52°48'32.9"W

Location: Red Head Cove
Access: Grounds open, tower closed

Name: Bear Cove Point Lighthouse
Opened: 1960s
Coordinates: 46°56'25.9"N 52°53'34.4"W

Location: Renews
Access: Closed

Name: Colombier Islands
Opened: 1971
Coordinates: 47°35'30.9"N 58°53'50.3"W

Location: Burnt Islands
Access: Grounds open, tower closed

Name: Conche
Opened: 1914
Coordinates: 50°53'09.0"N 55°53'45.8"W

Location: Conche
Access: Grounds open, tower closed

Name: Green Island (Fortune Bay)
Opened: 1993
Coordinates: 46°52'47.0"N 56°05'08.5"W

Location: Fortune Bay
Access: Grounds open, tower closed

Name: La Haye Point
Opened: 1990s
Coordinates: 46°54'15.6"N 53°36'58.8"W

Location: Point La Haye
Access: Grounds open, tower closed

Name: Marticot Island
Opened: 1990s
Coordinates: 47°19'36.8"N 54°34'52.8"W

Location: Great Paradise
Access: Closed

Name: North Penguin Island
Opened: 1890
Coordinates: 49°26'58.9"N 53°48'43.5"W

Location: Musgrave Harbour
Access: Closed

Name: Pass Island
Opened: 1879
Coordinates: 47°29'24.3"N 56°11'46.7"W

Location: Seal Cove
Access: Grounds open, tower closed

Name: Saddle Island (Red Bay)
Opened: Red Bay
Coordinates: 51°43'28.6"N 56°26'09.0"W

Location: Red Bay
Access: Grounds open, tower closed

Name: Salmon Point
Opened: 1989s
Coordinates: 47°37'03.0"N 56°12'01.4"W

Location: McCallum
Access: Grounds open, tower closed

Name: Surgeon Cove Point
Opened: 1911
Coordinates: 49°31'05.3"N 55°07'05.5"W

Location: Fortune Harbour
Access: Grounds open, tower closed

Tours

Labrador Tour

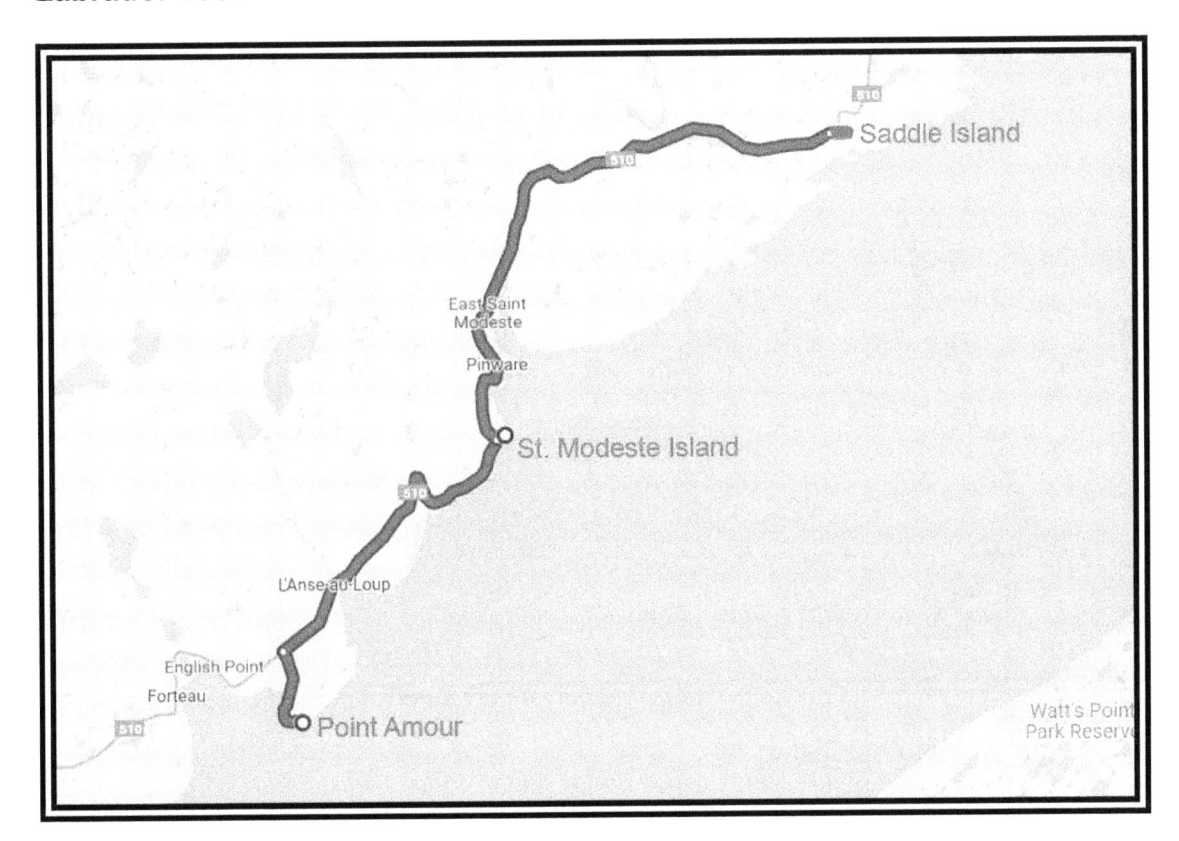

3 Lighthouses, 1 hour driving

Point Amour   51°27'37.7"N 56°51'29.3"W
St. Modeste Island   51°35'43.0"N 56°42'02.0"W
Saddle Island   51°43'28.6"N 56°26'09.0"W

Northern Newfoundland Tour1

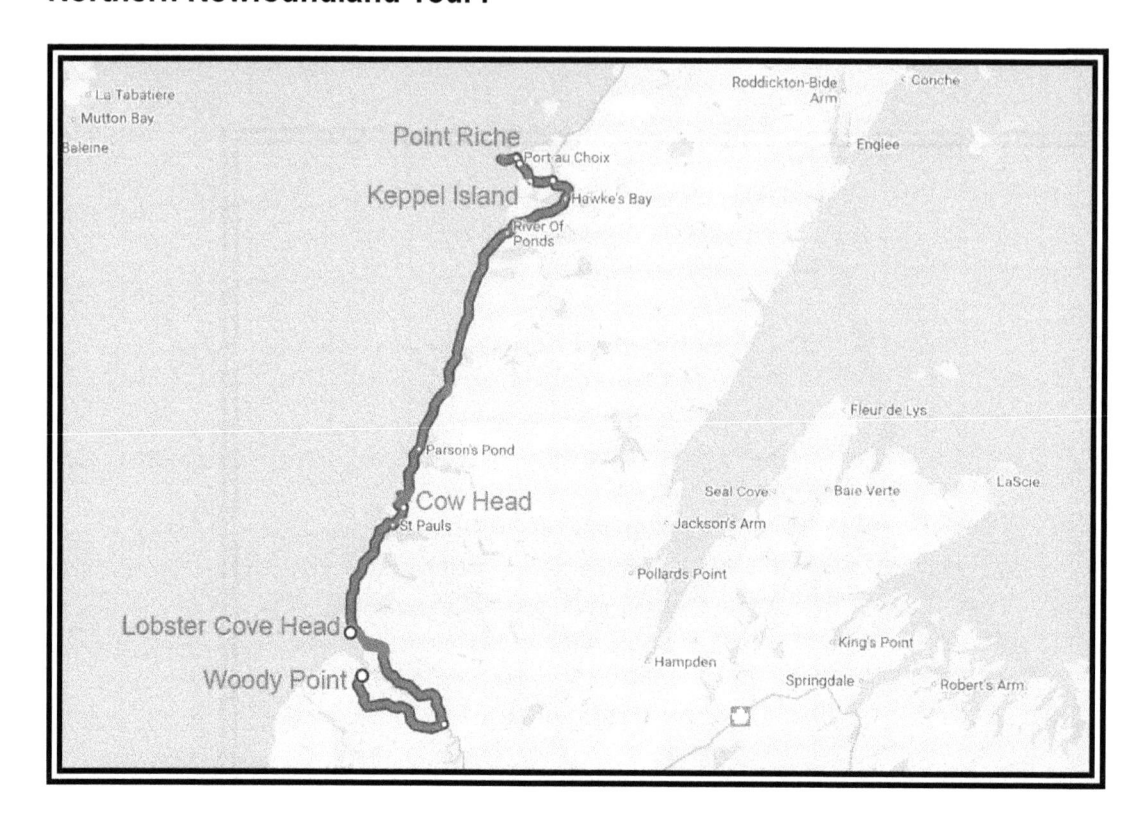

5 lighthouses, 3 hours 15 minutes driving

Woody Point	49°30'17.5"N 57°54'46.4"W
Lobster Cove Head	49°36'10.3"N 57°57'21.3"W
Cow Head	49°55'09.8"N 57°49'26.3"W
Keppel Island	50°37'58.9"N 57°19'19.9"W
Point Riche	50°41'54.6"N 57°24'36.8"W

Northern Newfoundland Tour2

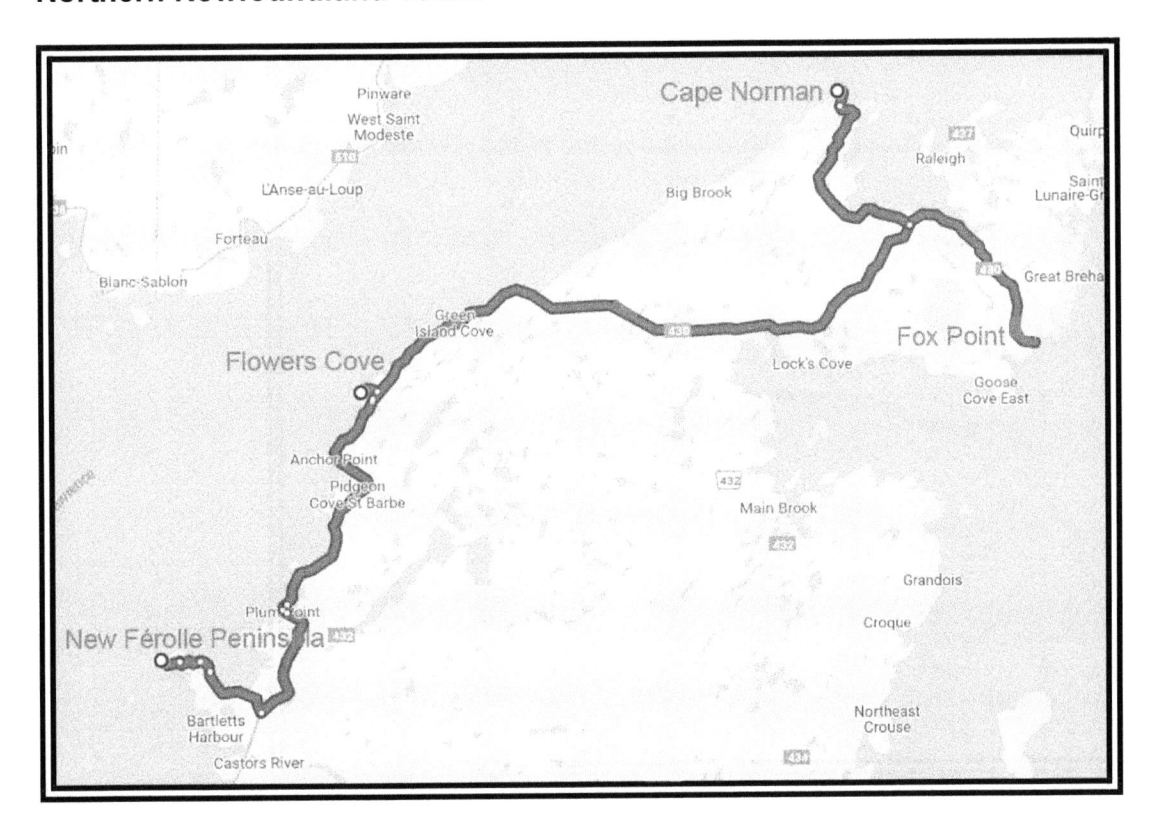

4 lighthouses, 4 hours 15 minutes driving

New Férolle Peninsula	51°01'22.1"N 57°05'44.5"W
Flowers Cove	51°18'30.1"N 56°44'55.2"W
Cape Norman	51°37'41.7"N 55°54'21.2"W
Fox Point	51°21'22.0"N 55°33'18.3"W

Northern Newfoundland Tour3

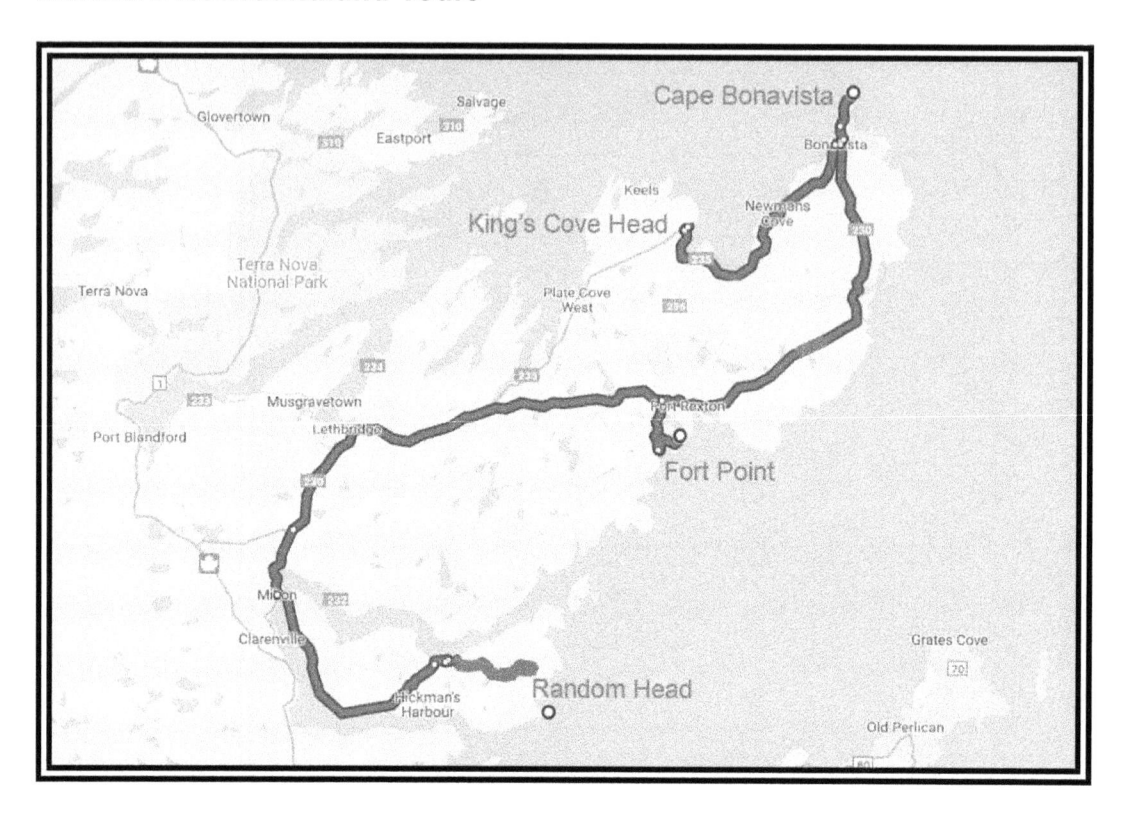

4 lighthouses, 3 hours 45 minutes driving

Random Head	48°05'41.1"N 53°32'43.1"W
Fort Point	48°21'55.0"N 53°20'42.0"W
Cape Bonavista	48°42'05.2"N 53°05'06.9"W
King's Cove Head	48°34'32.0"N 53°19'25.0"W

South Newfoundland Tour1

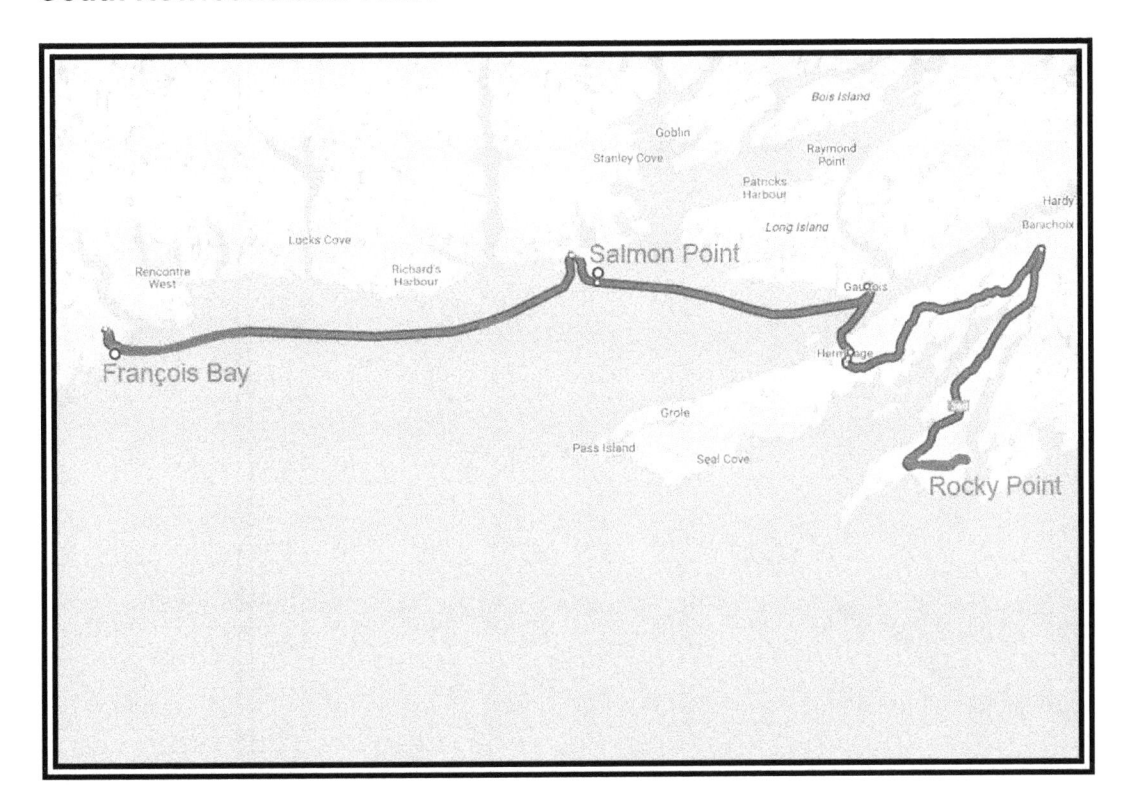

3 lighthouses, 5 hours driving

François Bay	47°33'35.7"N 56°44'02.1"W
Salmon Point	47°37'03.0"N 56°12'01.4"W
Rocky Point	47°28'46.3"N 55°47'34.4"W

South Newfoundland Tour2

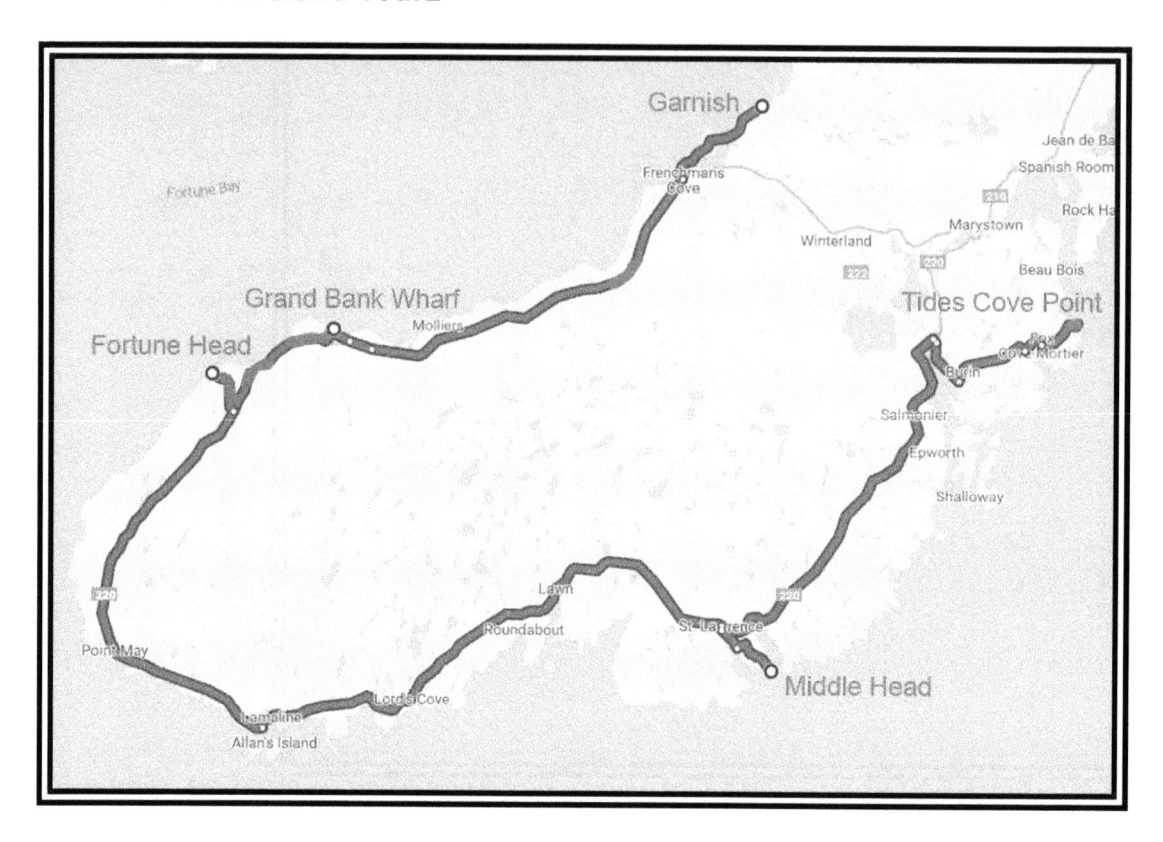

5 lighthouses, 3 hours driving

Garnish	47°14'10.2"N 55°21'30.6"W
Grand Bank Wharf	47°06'04.7"N 55°44'57.8"W
Fortune Head	47°04'27.7"N 55°51'33.2"W
Middle Head	46°53'52.8"N 55°20'51.2"W
Tides Cove Point	47°06'21.7"N 55°04'20.9"W

St. John's Tour

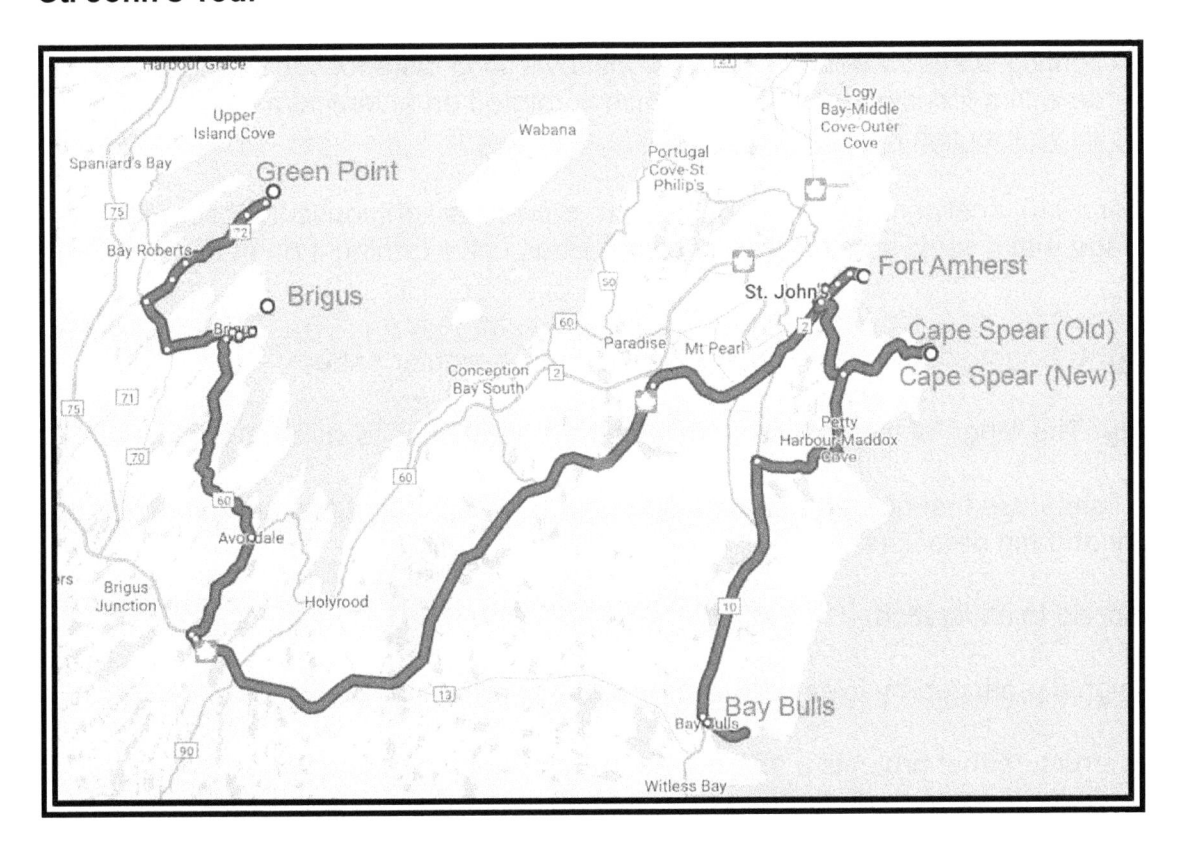

6 lighthouses, 2 hours 45 minutes driving

Green Point	47°36'41.4"N 53°10'36.1"W
Brigus	47°32'54.6"N 53°10'55.2"W
Fort Amherst	47°33'47.9"N 52°40'49.6"W
Cape Spear (Old)	47°31'11.8"N 52°37'24.0"W
Cape Spear (New)	
Bay Bulls	47°18'38.7"N 52°44'48.6"W

Glossary of Lighthouse Terms

Aerobeacon: A lighting system which creates a signal over long distances. It consists of a strong light source with a focusing mechanism which is rotated on a vertical axis. It has been used at airports as well as lighthouses.

Acetylene: After 1910, acetylene began to be used to power the lighthouse light source. It has the advantage that it could be stored on site with a sun valve turning it on at dusk and off at daybreak.

Alternating Light: A light source which changes colours in a regular pattern.

Arc of Visibility: The range of the horizon from which the lighthouse is visible from the sea.

Automated: A lighthouse that operates without a keeper. The light functions are controlled by timers, and light and fog detectors.

Beacon: A fixed aid to navigation.

Bell: A sound signal produced by fixed aids and by sea movement on buoys.

Breakwater: A structure that protects a shore area or harbour by blocking waves.

Bull's-eye Lens: A convex lens used to refract light.

Catwalk: An elevated walkway which allows the keeper to move in the lantern room in towers built in the sea.

Characteristic: The distinct pattern of the flashing light or foghorn blast which allows seamen to distinguish which light station it is coming from.

Chariot: A wheeled assembly at the bottom of a Fresnel lens which is rotated around a circular track.

Clockwork Mechanism: Early lighthouses had a series of gears, pulleys and weights, which had to be wound on a recurring basis by the keepers.

Cottage Style Lighthouse: A lighthouse made up of a keeper's residence with a light on top.

Crib: A base structure filled with stone which acted as the foundation for the structure built on top.

Daymark: A unique colour pattern that identifies a specific lighthouse during the day.

Decommissioned: A lighthouse that has discontinued operating as a aid to navigation.

Diaphone: A sound signal produced by a slotted piston moved by compressed air.

Directional Light: A light which marks the direction to be followed.

Eclipse: The interval between light flashed or foghorn blasts.

Fixed Light: A light shining continuously without periods of eclipse or darkness.

Flashing Light: Alight pattern distinguished by periods of eclipse or darkness.

Focal Plane: The path of a beam of light emitted from a lighthouse. The height from the center of the beam to the sea is known as the height of the focal plane.

Fog Detector: A device used to automatically determine conditions which may reduce visibility and the need to start a sound signal.

Fog Signal: An audible device such as a bell or horn that warns seamen during period of fog when the light would be ineffective.

Fresnel Lens: An optic system composed of a convex lens and prisms which concentrate the light beam through a series of prisms. The design was produced by Augustin Fresnel in the 1800s.

Geographic Range: The longest distance the curvature of the earth allows an object of a certain height to be seen.

Isophase Light: A light in which the duration of light and darkness are equal.

Keeper: The person responsible for the maintenance and operation of the lighthouse.

Lamp and Reflector: A lamp and polished mirror used before the invention of more effective optic systems such as the Fresnel lens.

Lantern: A glass covered space at the top of the lighthouse tower, which housed the lighting equipment.

Lens: The glass optical system used to concentrate and direct the light.

Light Sector: The arc over which a light can be seen from the sea.

Lightship: A ship that served as a lighthouse.

Light Station: The lighthouse tower as well as any outbuildings such as the keeper's quarters, fog-signal building, fuel storage building and boathouse.

Nautical Mile: A unit of distance which is the average distance on the Earth's surface represented by one minute of latitude. It is equal to 1.1508 statute miles and mainly used at sea.

Nominal Range: The distance a light can be seen in good weather.

Occulting Light: A light in which the period of light is longer than the period of darkness and in which the intervals of darkness are all equal. Also known as an eclipsing light.

Order: A description of the power of the Fresnel lens ranging from one to seven from stronger to weaker.

Parabolic Reflector: A metal bowl shaped to a parabolic curve which reflects a lamp's light from it's center.

Parapet: A railed walkway which surrounds the lamp room.

Period: The total time for one cycle of the pattern of the light or sound signal.

Pharologist: A person with an interest in lighthouses.

Range Lights: Two lights which form a range provide direction to mariners for safe passage. They are described as the Front and Rear Lighthouses or the Inner and Outer. The front range light is lower than the rear, and when they align, the ship is in the proper position.

Revetment: A bank of stone laid to protect a structure against erosion from waves.

Revolving Light: A flash produced by the rotation of a Fresnel lens.

Riprap: Broken rocks or stone placed to help prevent erosion.

Sector: The portion of the sea lit by a sector light.

Skeleton Tower: Towers consisting of four or more braced feet with a beacon on top. They have little resistance to the wind and waves, and bear up well in a storm.

Solar-powered Optic: Many automated lights are run on solar powered batteries.

Spider Lamp: A brass container holding oil and solid wicks.

Tender: A ship which services lighthouses.

Ventilator: Opening' at the top of a lighthouse tower to provide heat exhaust and air flow within the tower.

Wick Solid: A solid cord which draws fuel to the flame in spider lamps.

Photo Credits

Alessio Damato; Coruna torre de hercules; **Canadian Coast Guard**; Cabot island, Dawsons Point, Double Island, Green Island, Gull Island, Little Denier Island, Miiddle Head, Northwest Head, Offer Wadham Island, St Jacques Island, Belle Island South Lower; **Colleen Martin**; Fortune Head, Grand Bank; **Fisheries and Oceans**; Bacalhao Island, Baccalieu Island, Broad Cove, Burnt Point, English Harbour West, François Bay, Garnish, Keppel Island, Manuel Island, Peckford Island, Random Head, Rocky Point, Boar Island; **John King**; Kings Cove Head; **Larry Lamsa**; Long Point; **Loozrboy**; Cape Spear Old; **Magicpiano**; Cow Head; **Michel Rathwell;** Cape St. Mary, Lobster Cove Head; **Mike Vancouver**; Channel Head; **Parks Canada**; Cape Pine; **Paul Okeefe**; Sandy Point Island; **Psythe**; Woody Point; **Ryan Patey**; Cape Bauld, **Thiersch**; Pharos; **Timothy Neesam**; Puffin Island

All other images by the author

The Photographer's and Explorer's Series

Unless noted, there are Print and eBook editions available for the following.

Birds
Birding Guide to Orkney
Guide to Photographing Birds

Covered Bridges
Alabama Covered Bridges (eBook)
California Covered Bridges (eBook)
Connecticut Covered Bridges (eBook)
Covered Bridges of Canada
Georgia Covered Bridges (eBook)
Indiana Covered Bridges
Maine Covered Bridges (eBook)
Massachusetts Covered Bridges (eBook)
Michigan Covered Bridges (eBook)
New Brunswick Covered Bridges
New England Covered Bridges
Covered Bridges of the Mid-Atlantic
New Hampshire Covered Bridges
New York Covered Bridges
Covered Bridges of the North
Ohio's Covered Bridges
Oregon Covered Bridges
The Covered Bridges of Kentucky (eBook)
Covered Bridges of the South
The Covered Bridges of Kentucky and Tennessee
The Covered Bridges of Tennessee (eBook)
Vermont's Covered Bridges
The Covered Bridges of Virginia (eBook)
The Covered Bridges of Virginia and West Virginia
Washington Covered Bridges (eBook)
The Covered Bridges of West Virginia (eBook)

Lighthouses
Maine Lighthouses
New Brunswick Lighthouses
Prince Edward Island Lighthouses
Ontario Lighthouses
Orkney and Shetland Lighthouses (eBook)
Lighthouses of Scotland

Old Mills
Ontario's Old Mills

Waterfalls
Ontario Waterfalls

Index

Admiral's Point	41
Bacalhao Island	10
Baccalieu Island	11
Baccalieu Island Southwest Point	77
Bay Bulls	12
Bear Cove Point	77
Bell Island	13
Belle Island North End	14
Belle Island South End Lower	15
Belle Island South End Upper	15
Boar Island	16
Brigus	17
Broad Cove Point Range Front	18
Burnt Point	19
Cabot Islands	20
Camp Islands	21
Cape Anguille	22
Cape Bauld	23
Cape Bonavista	24
Cape Norman	25
Cape Pine	26
Cape Race	27
Cape Ray	28
Cape Spear (new)	29
Cape Spear (old)	30
Cape St Francis	31
Cape St. John	49
Cape St. Mary's	32
Channel Head	33
Colombier Islands	77
Conche	77
Cow Head	34
Dawson Point	35
Double Island	36
English Harbour West	37
Fermuse	77
Ferryland Head	38
Fishing Point	43
Flowers Cove	39
Fort Amherst	40
Fort Point	41
Fortune Head	42

Fox Point	43
François Bay	44
Garnish	45
Grand Bank Wharf	46
Green Island (Catalina)	47
Green Island (Fortune Bay)	77
Green Point	48
Gull Island	49
Hants Harbour	50
Harbour Breton	70
Harbour Point	51
Heart's Content	52
Keppel Island	53
Kings Cove Head	54
La Haye Point	77
Little Denier Island	55
Lobster Cove Head	56
Long Point	57
Manuel Island	58
Marticot Island	77
Middle Head	59
New Férolle Peninsula	60
North Penguin Island	77
Northwest Head	61
Offer Wadham Island	62
Pass Island	77
Peckford Island	63
Point Amour	64
Point Riche	65
Point Verde	66
Powles Head	67
Puffin Island	68
Ramea	61
Random Head Harbour	69
Red Bay	77
Rocky Point	70
Rose Blanche	71
Saddle Island	77
Salmon Point	78
Sandy Point	51
St. Jacques Island	72
St. Modeste Island	73
Surgeon Cove Point	78
Tides Cove Point	74

Twillingate	57
West Point	44
Westport Cove	75
Woody Point	76

www.ingramcontent.com/pod-product-compliance
Ingram Content Group UK Ltd.
Pitfield, Milton Keynes, MK11 3LW, UK
UKHW050437250225
455494UK00011B/104